World of Fairies

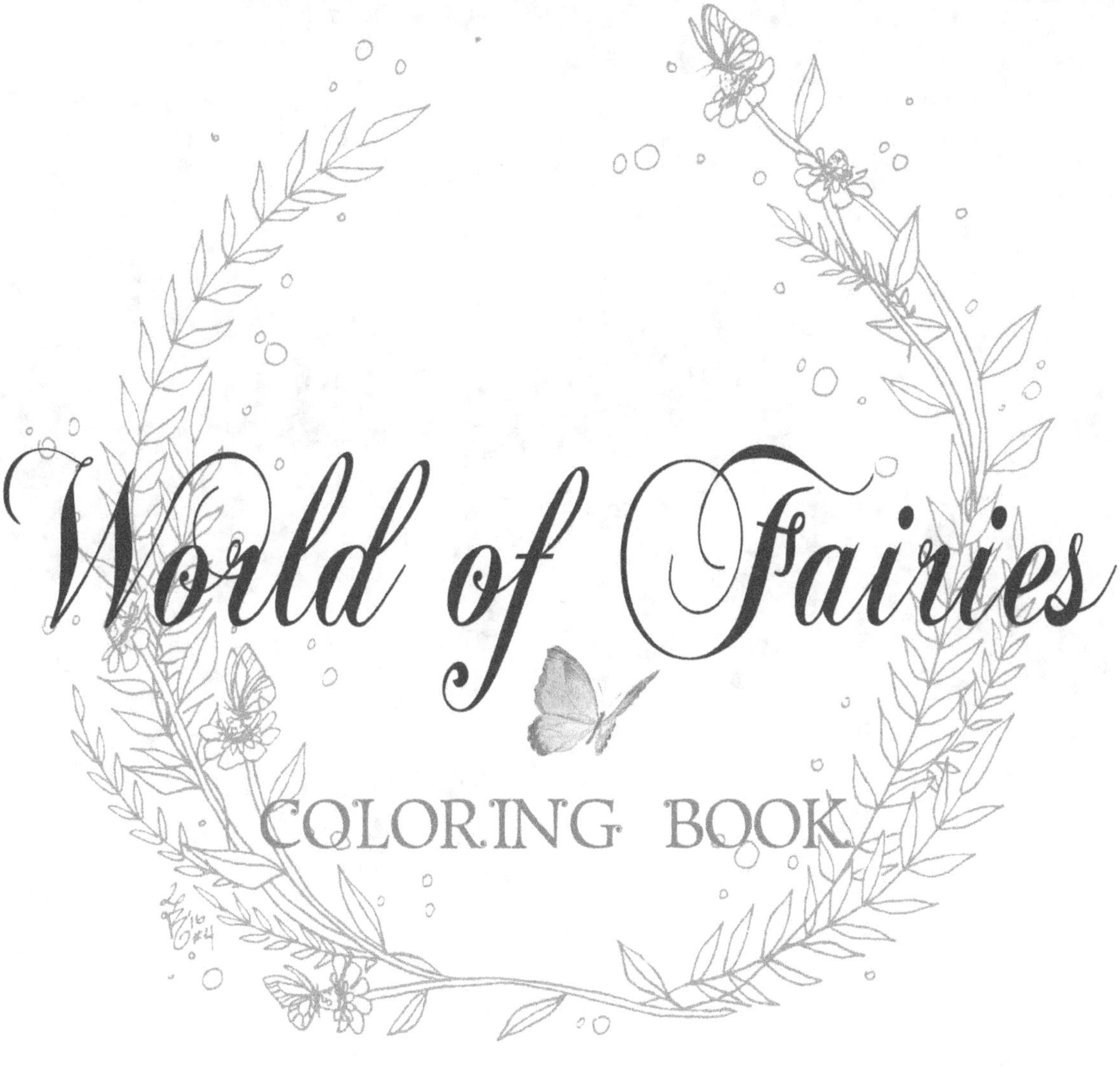

COLORING BOOK

Coloring Tips

Hand pick colored pencils from high quality brands instead of buying a large set filled with colors you may never use. Choose colors that YOU enjoy.

Burnish with a white colored pencil instead of a burnishing pencil to allow further color build up as you go.

Use light pressure to suggest a color or shadow; medium pressure to create a base for layering and blending; heavy pressure to give the color a solid feel, and to add burnishing.

Take your time and build up your colors slowly.

Use sandpaper to fashion extra sharp tips on your pencils.

Crosshatch your shadows in lightly first to help establish your light source.

Keep a variety of colored pencil types for different applications.

Use a kneaded eraser to pick up color, fading it back down.

Use a hard lead white pencil, newly sharpened, to pick up specks of pencil shavings from your creation.

Place a board between the pages to get a solid backing for your mark making.

GET LOST IN YOUR WORK.
ENJOY THE MOMENT!

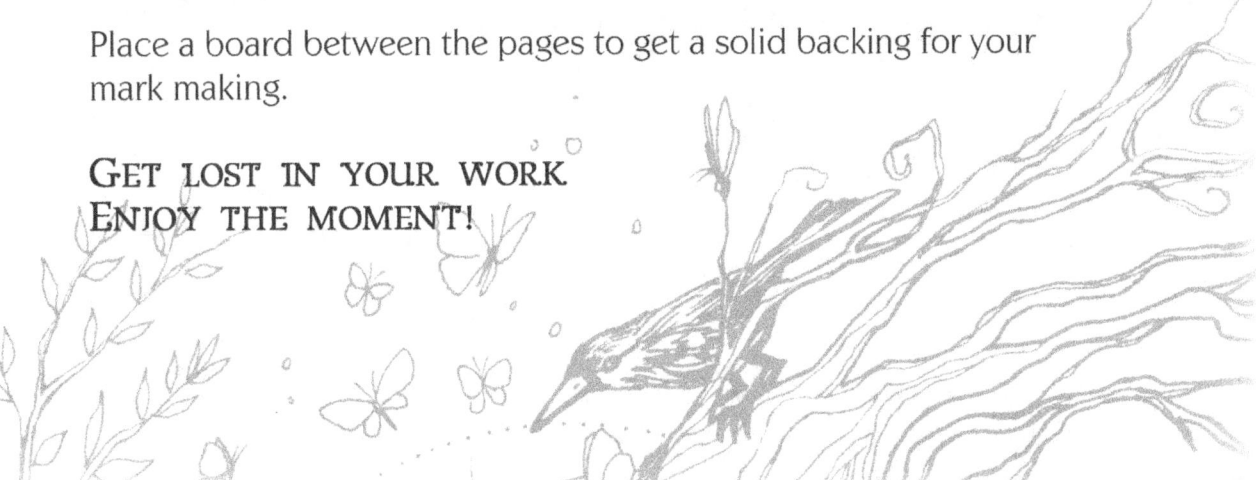

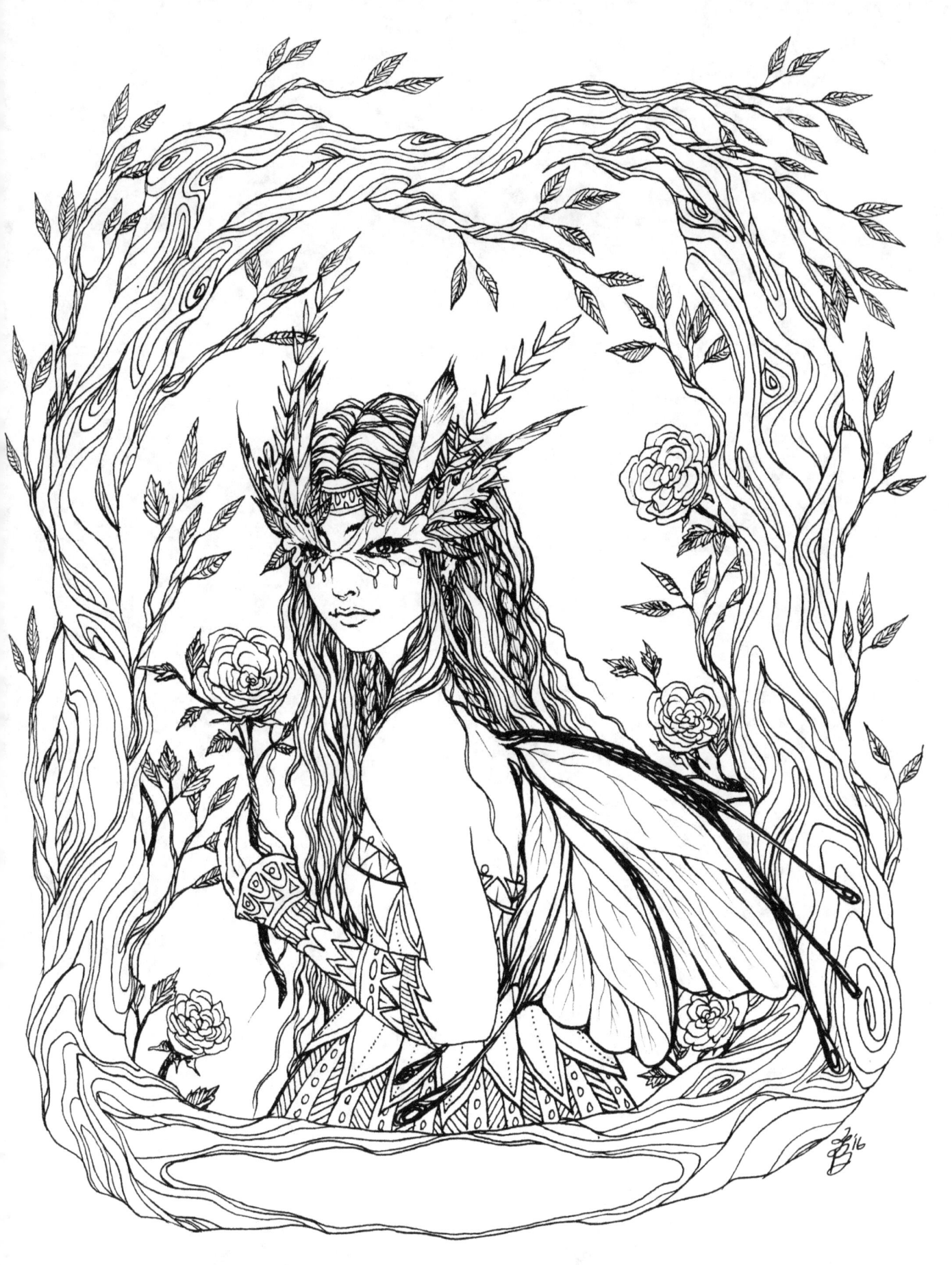

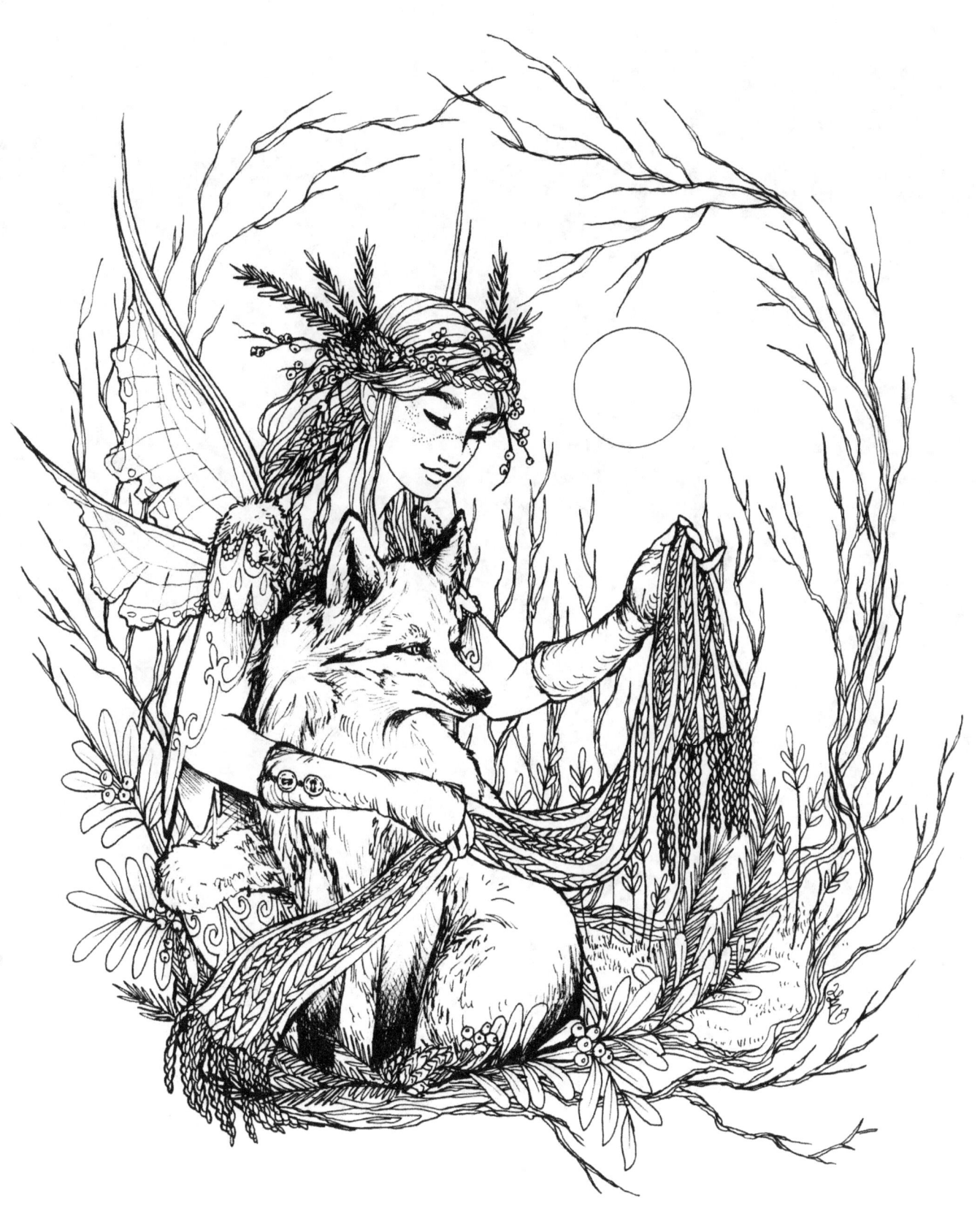

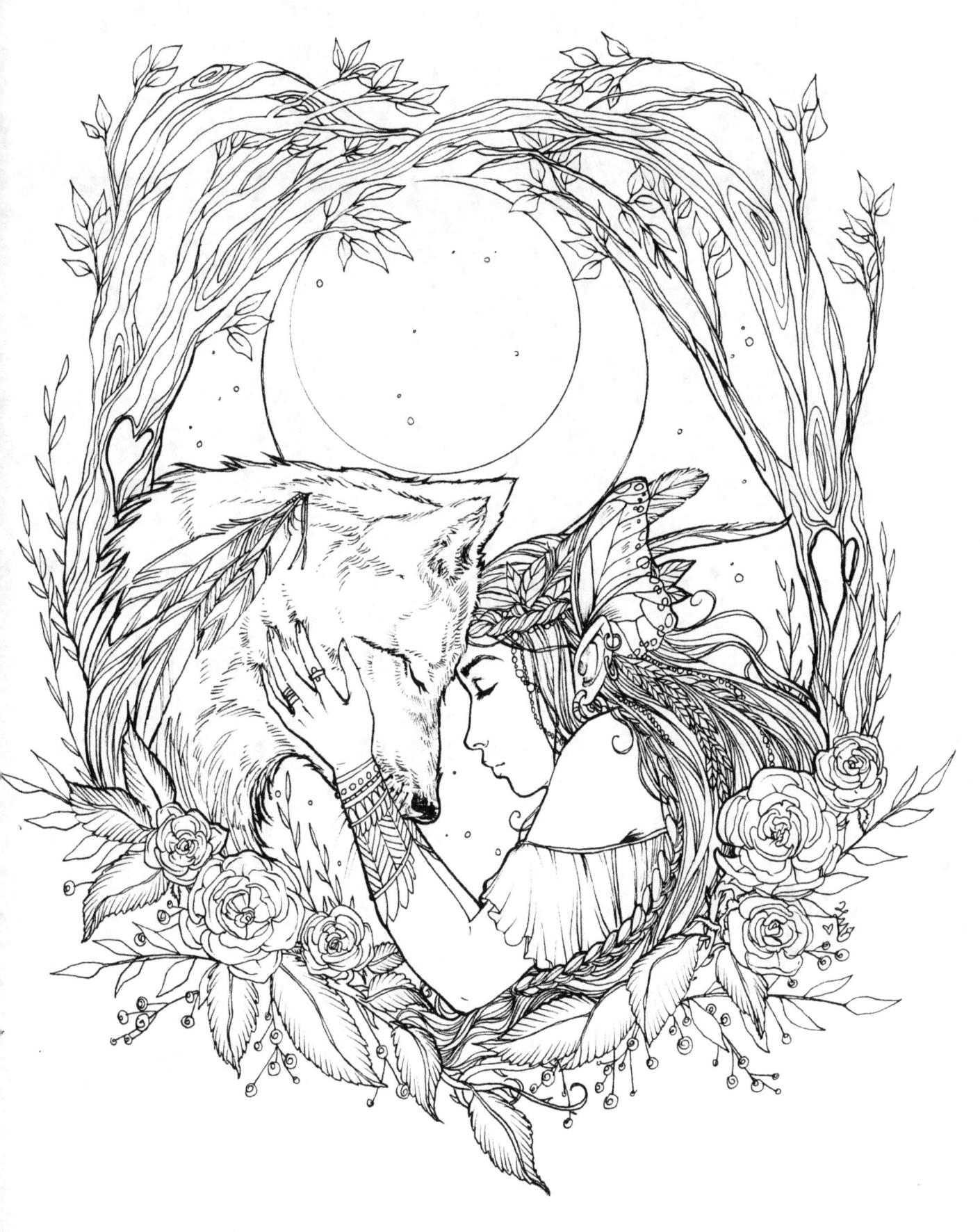

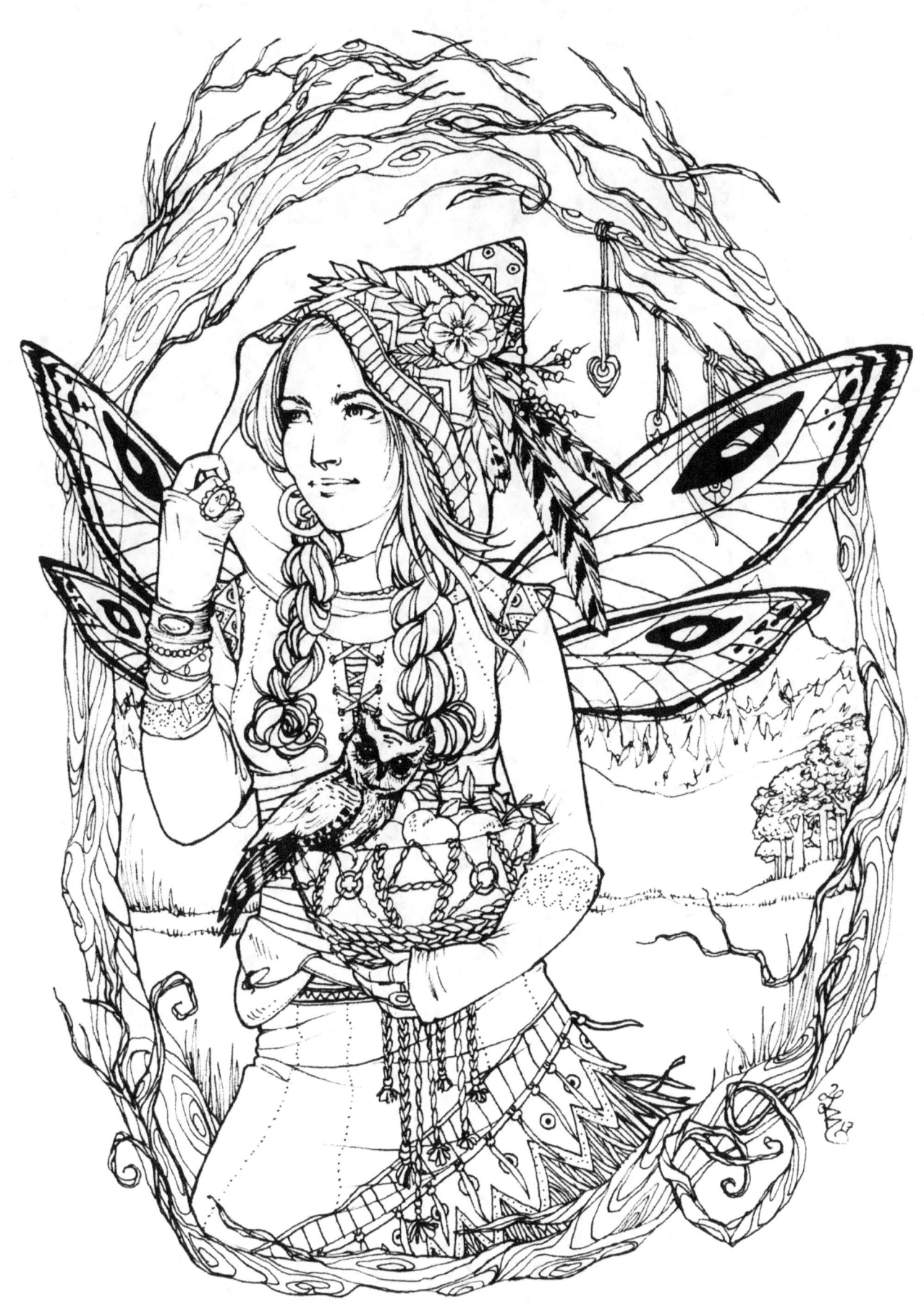

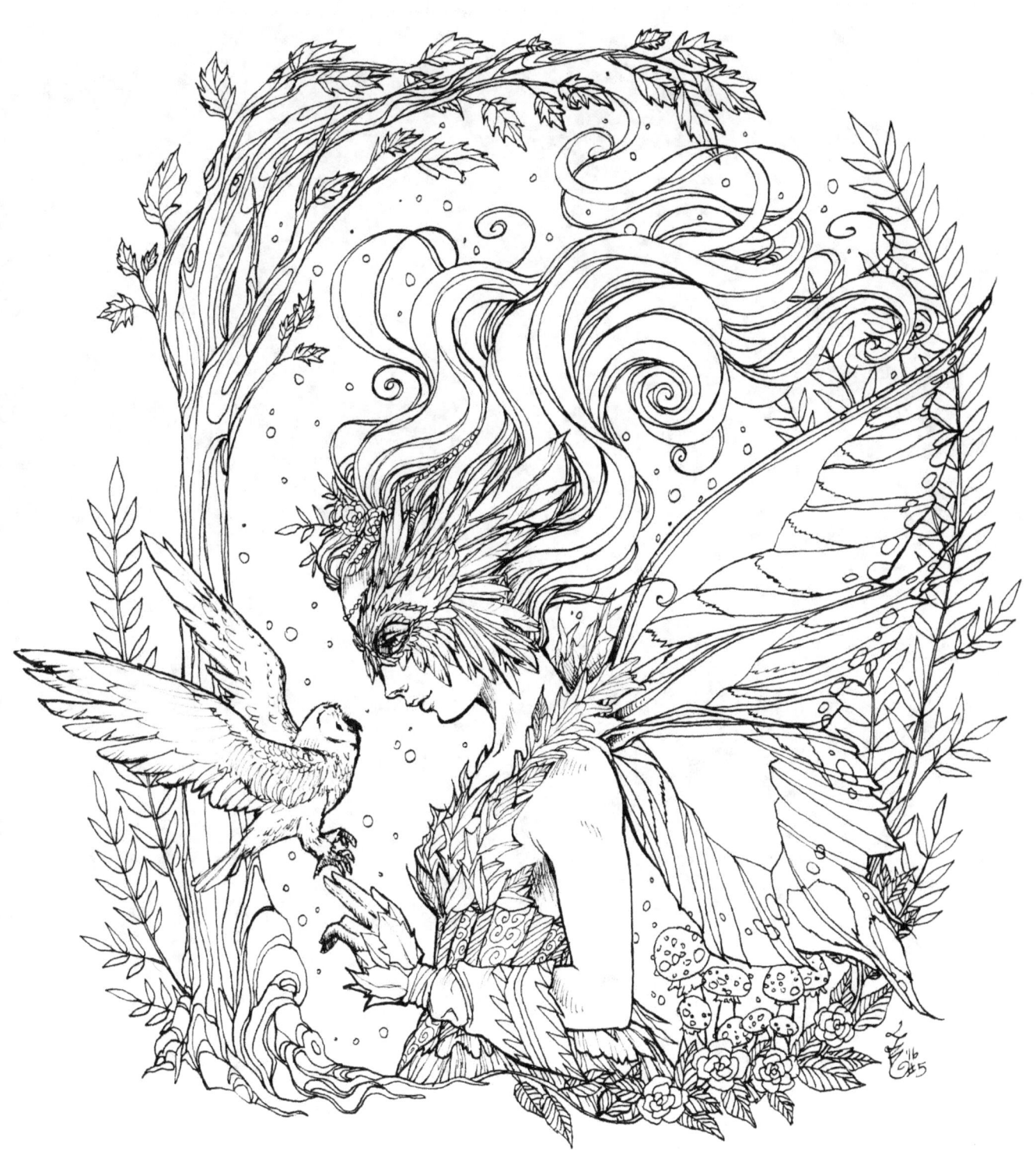

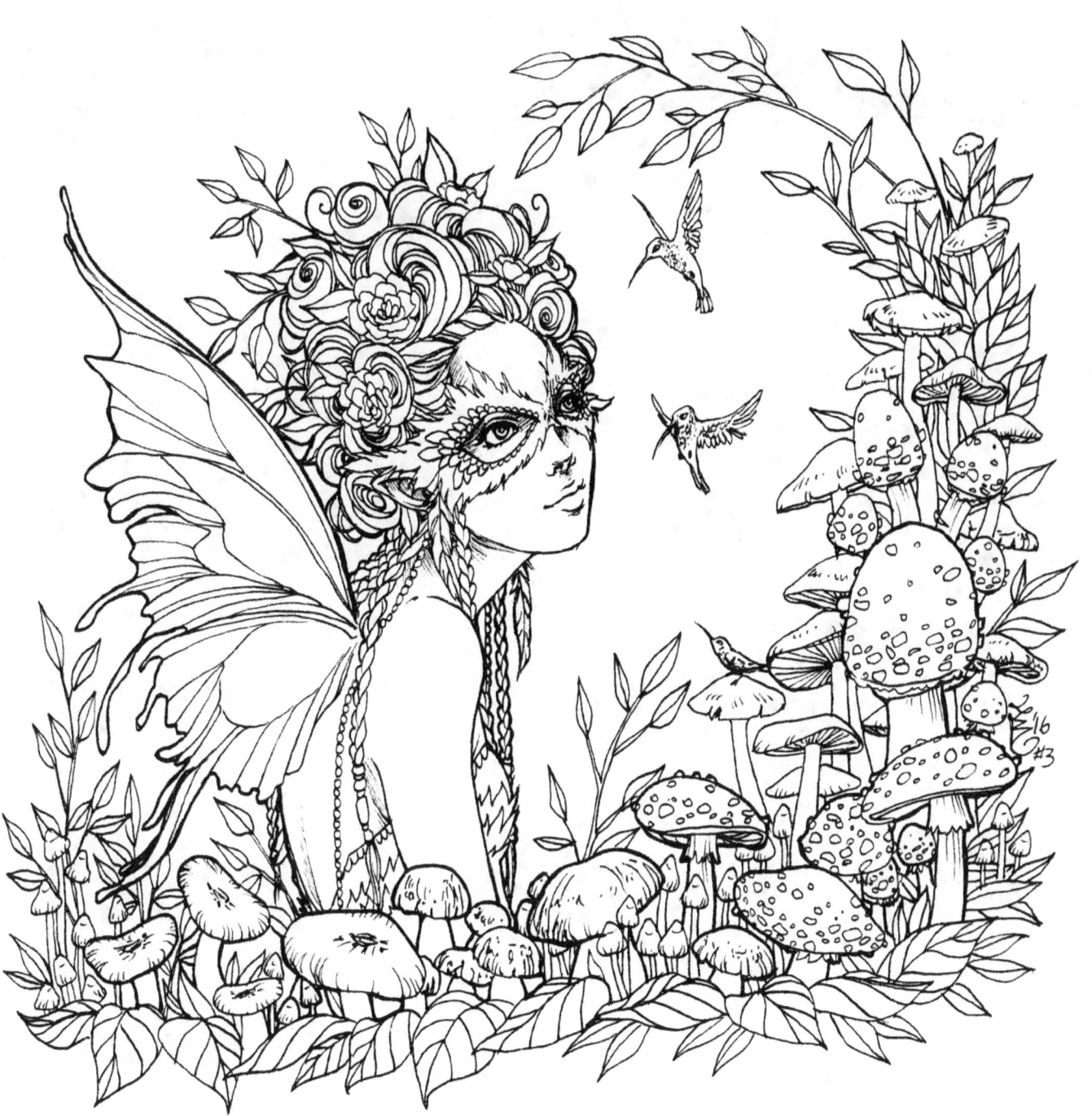

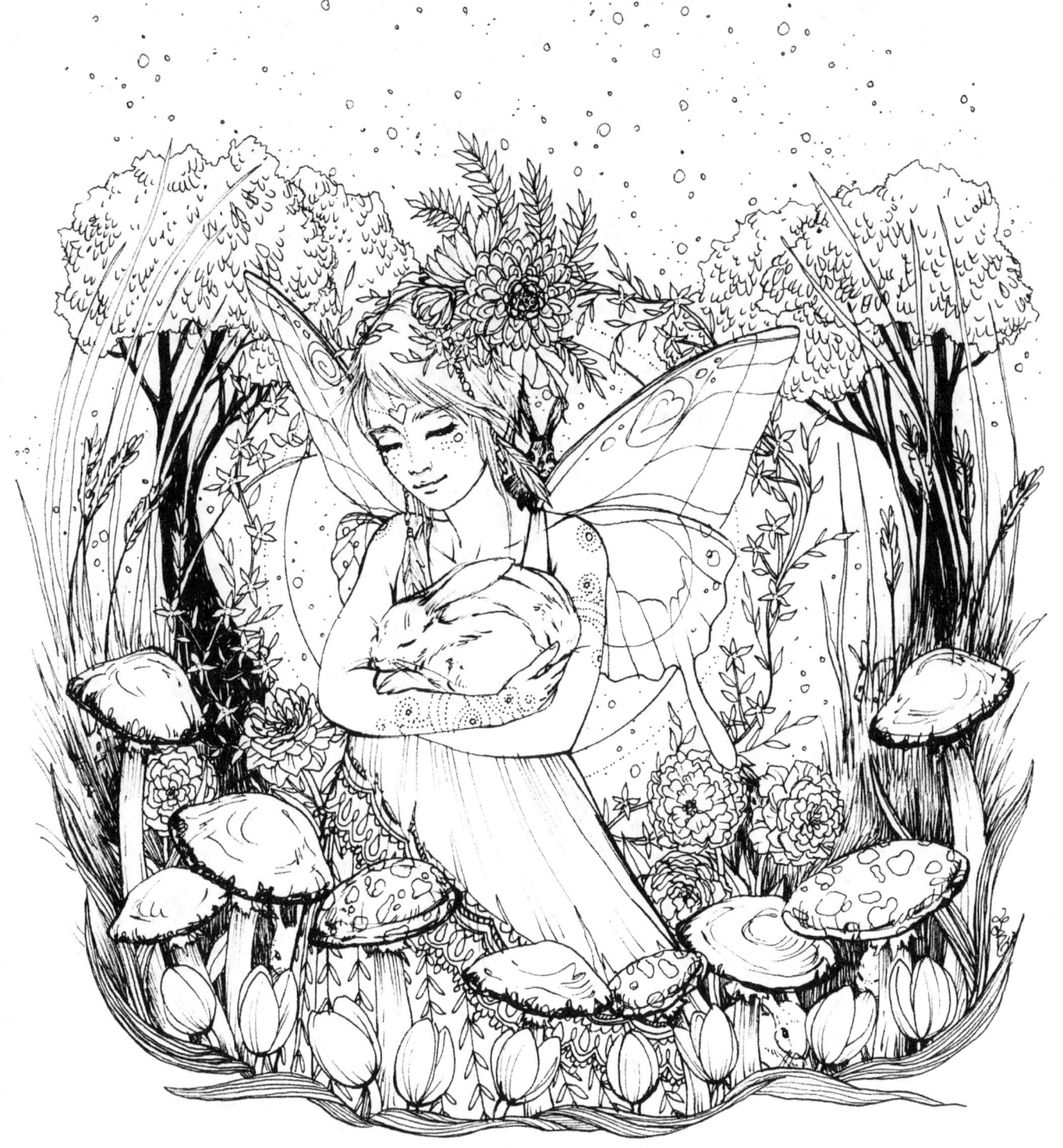

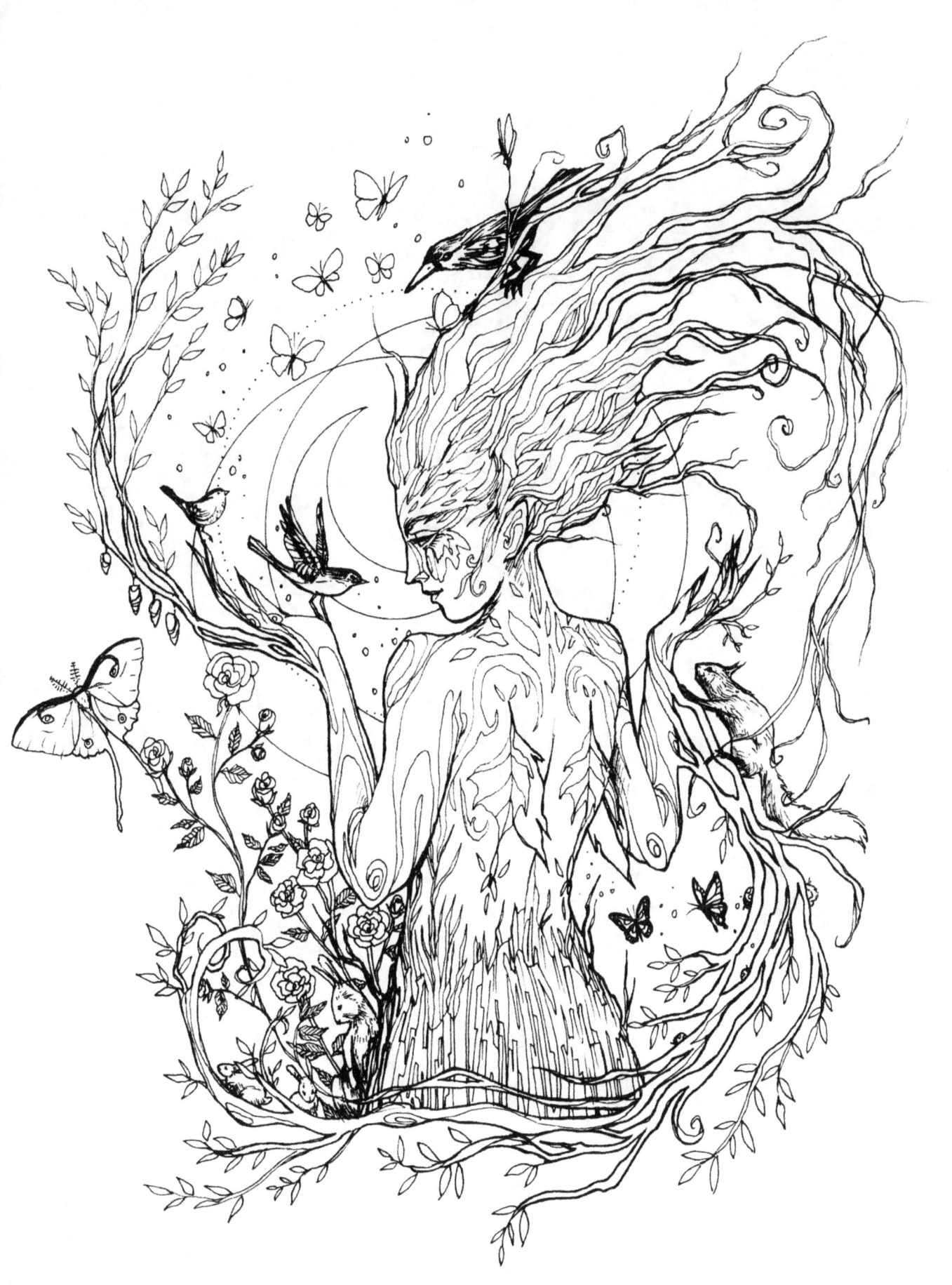

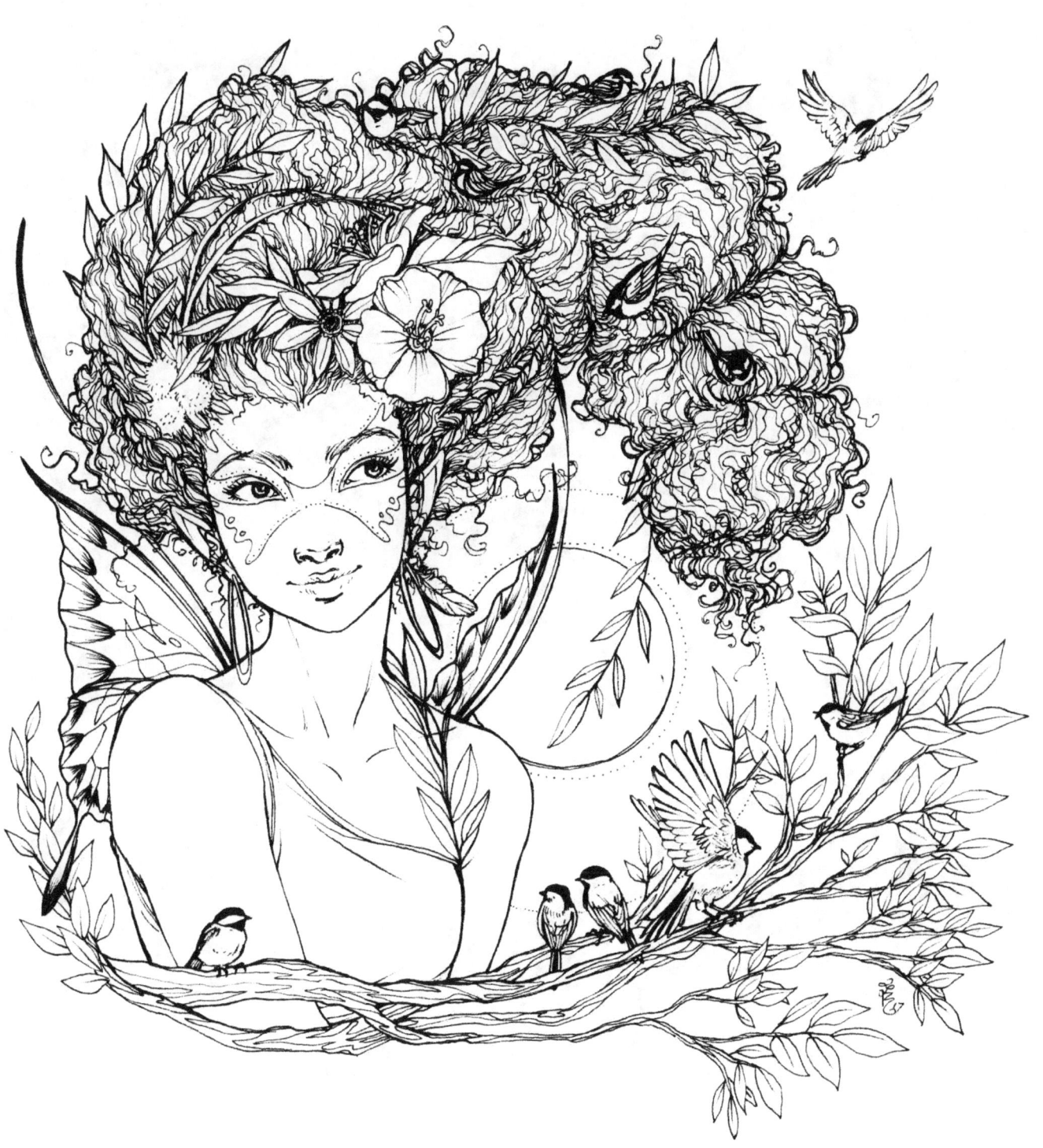

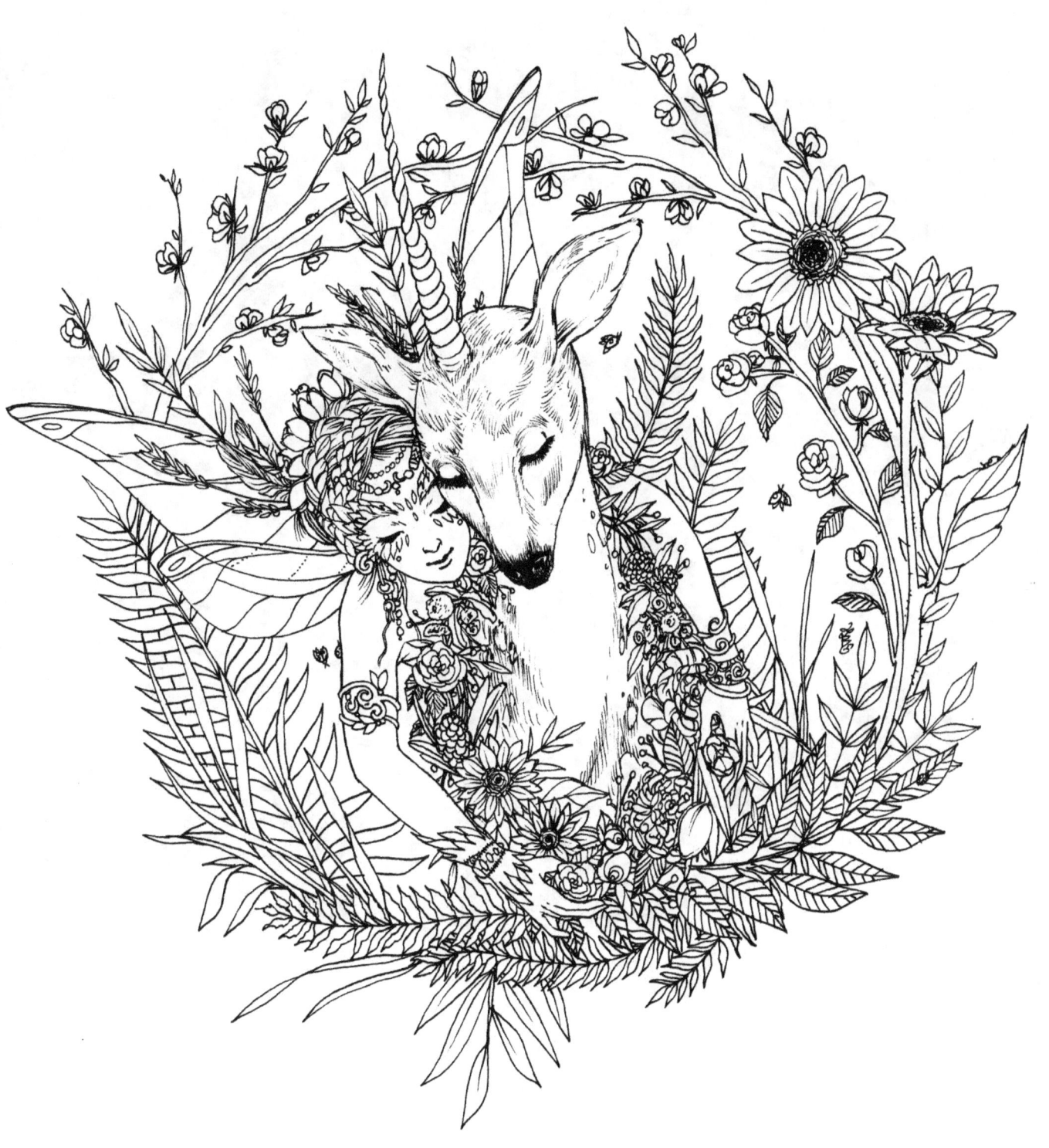

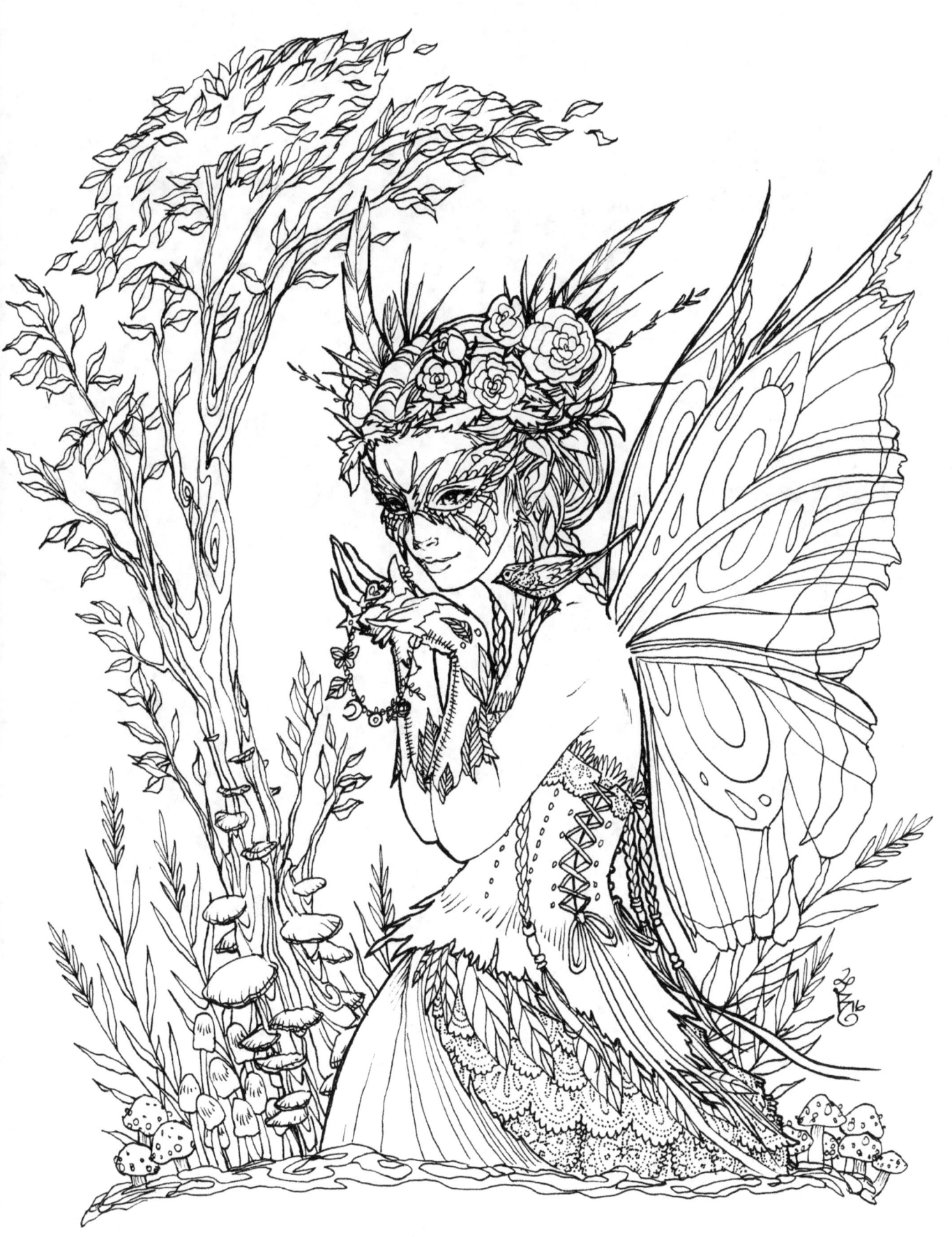

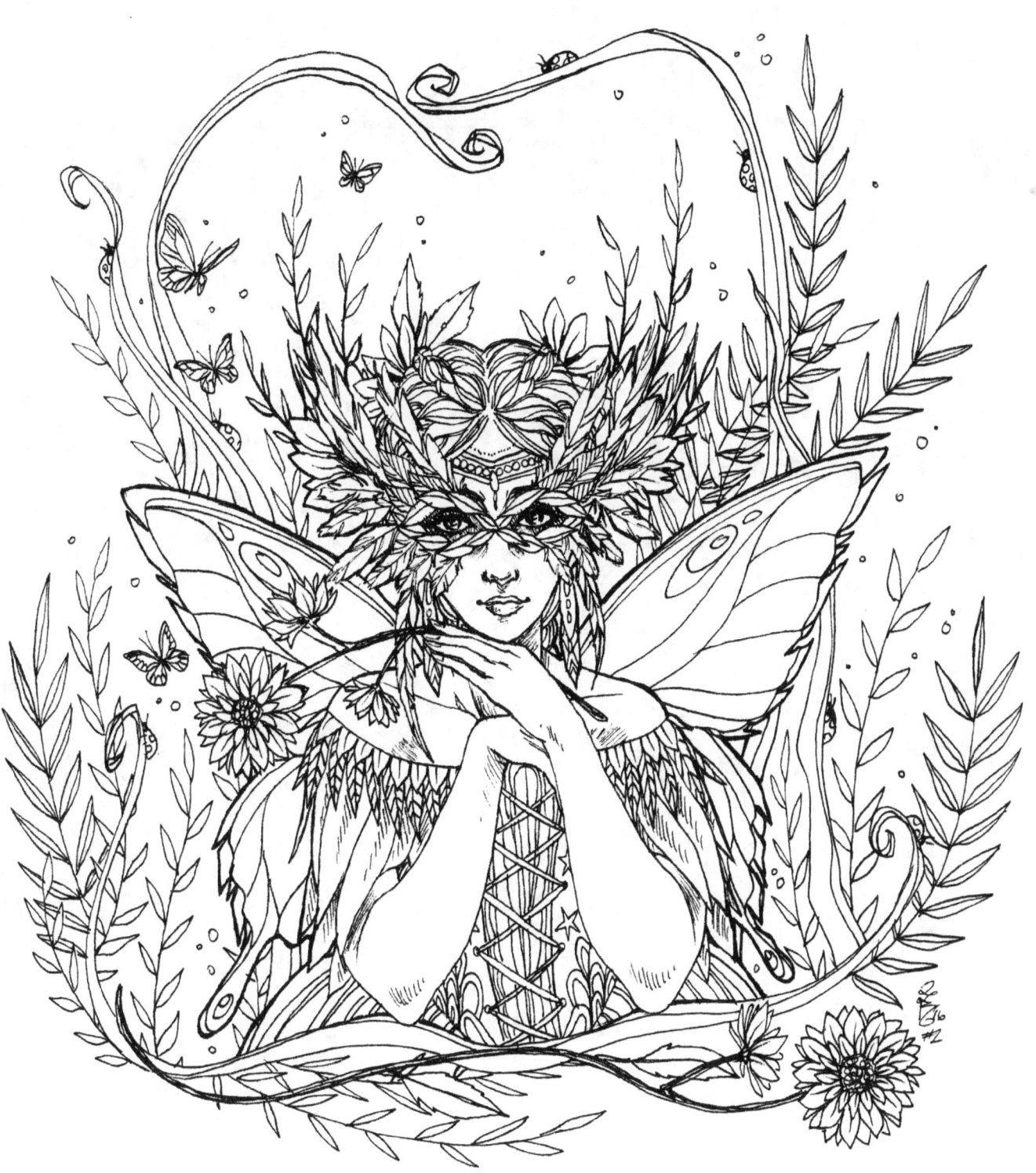

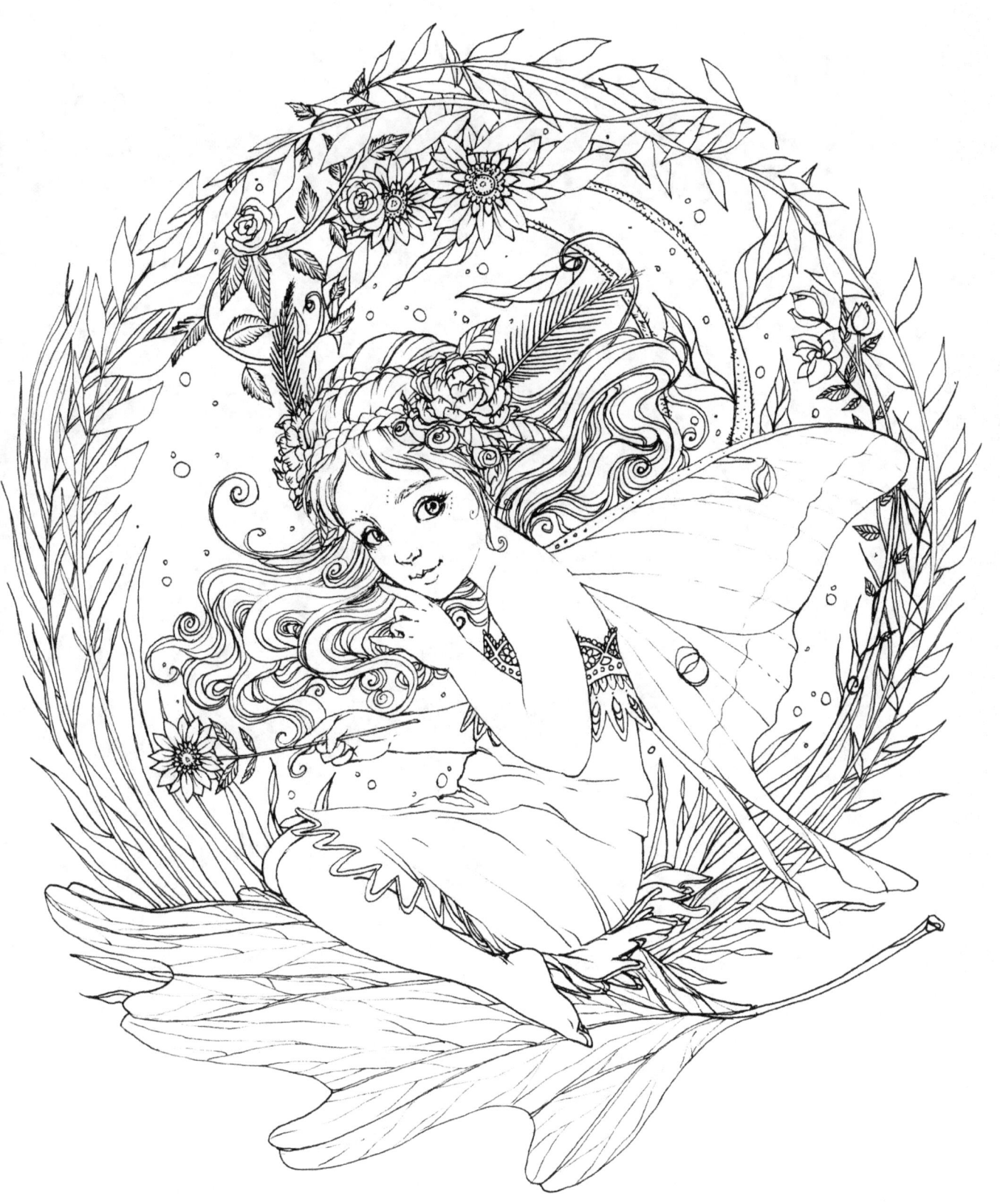

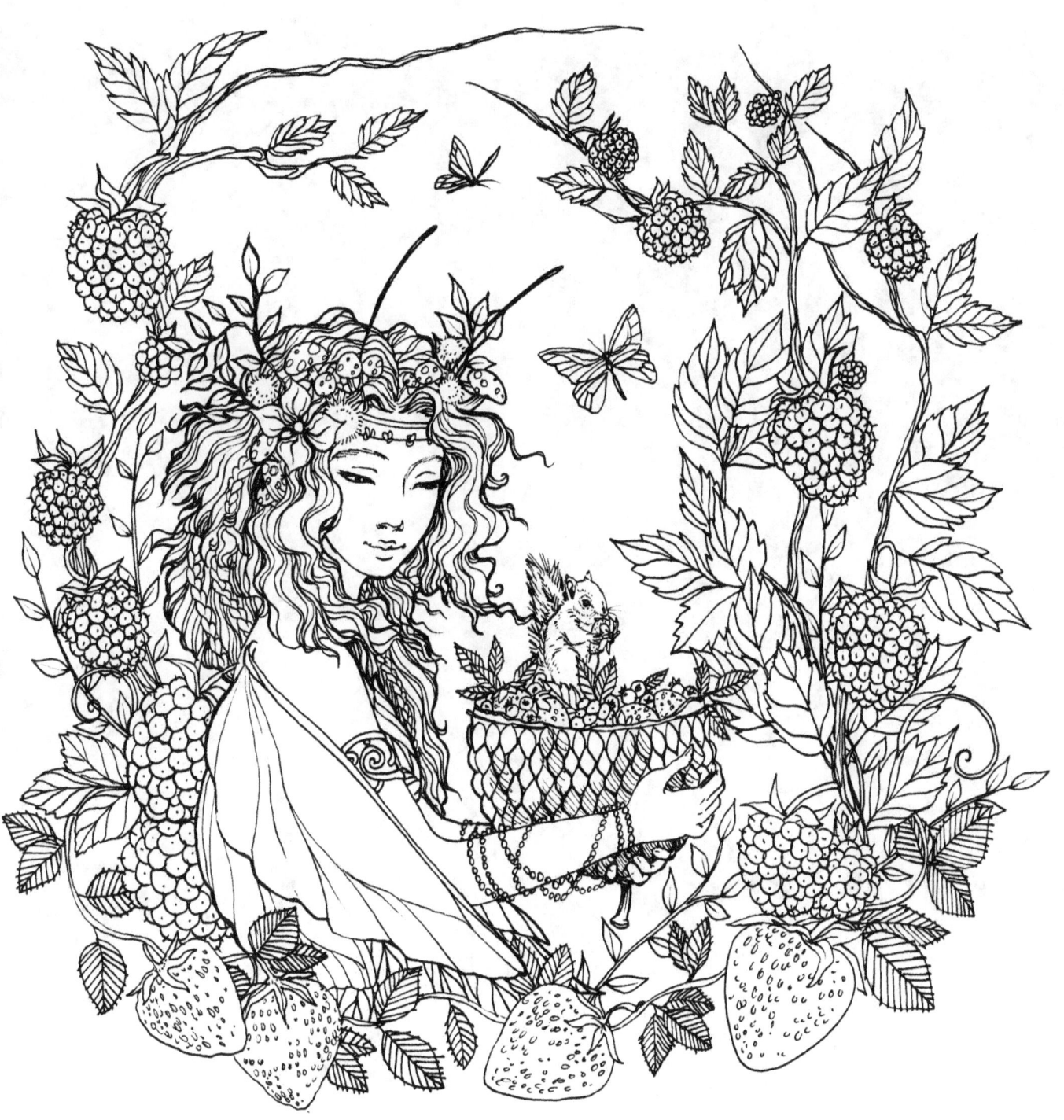

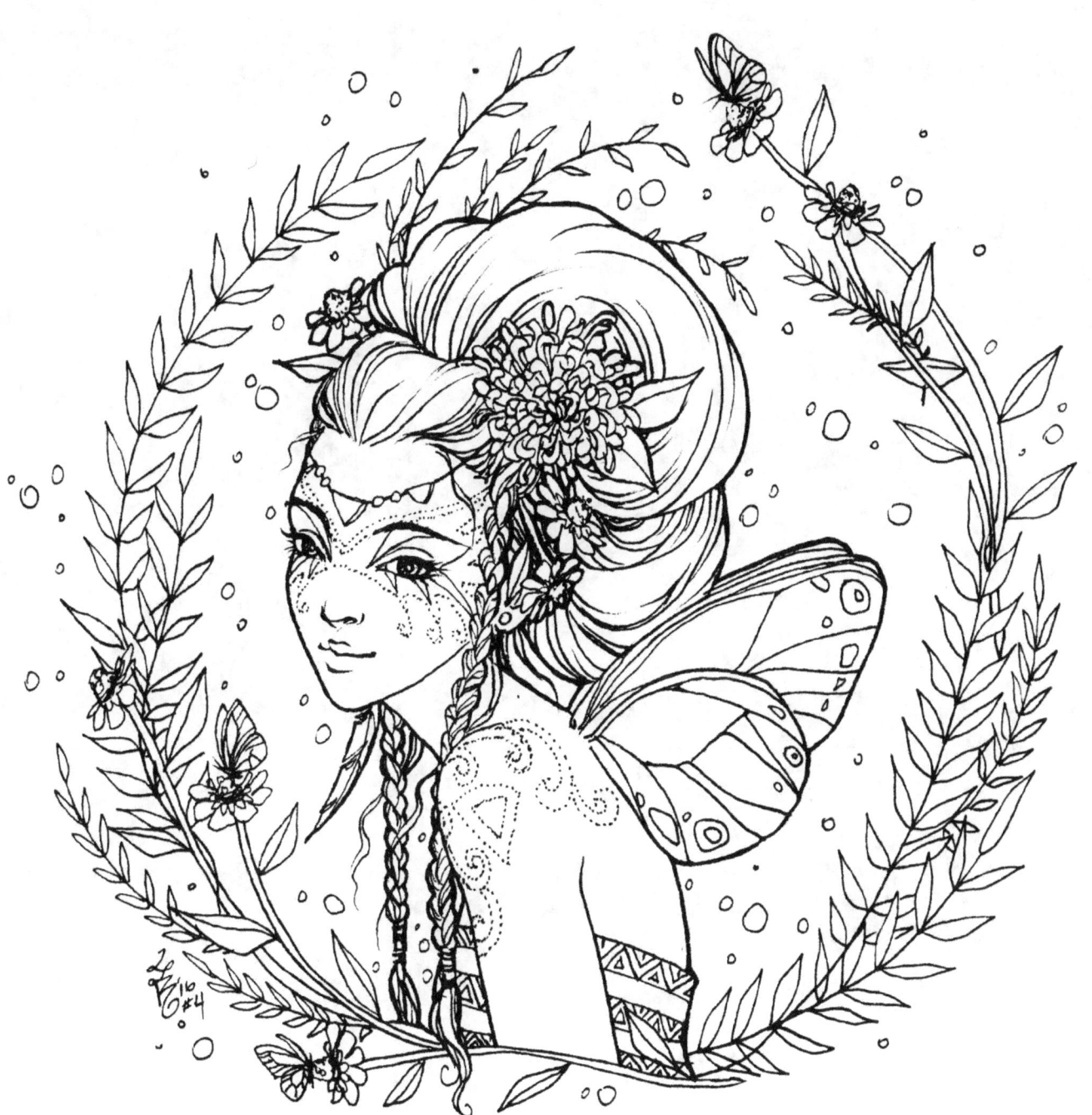

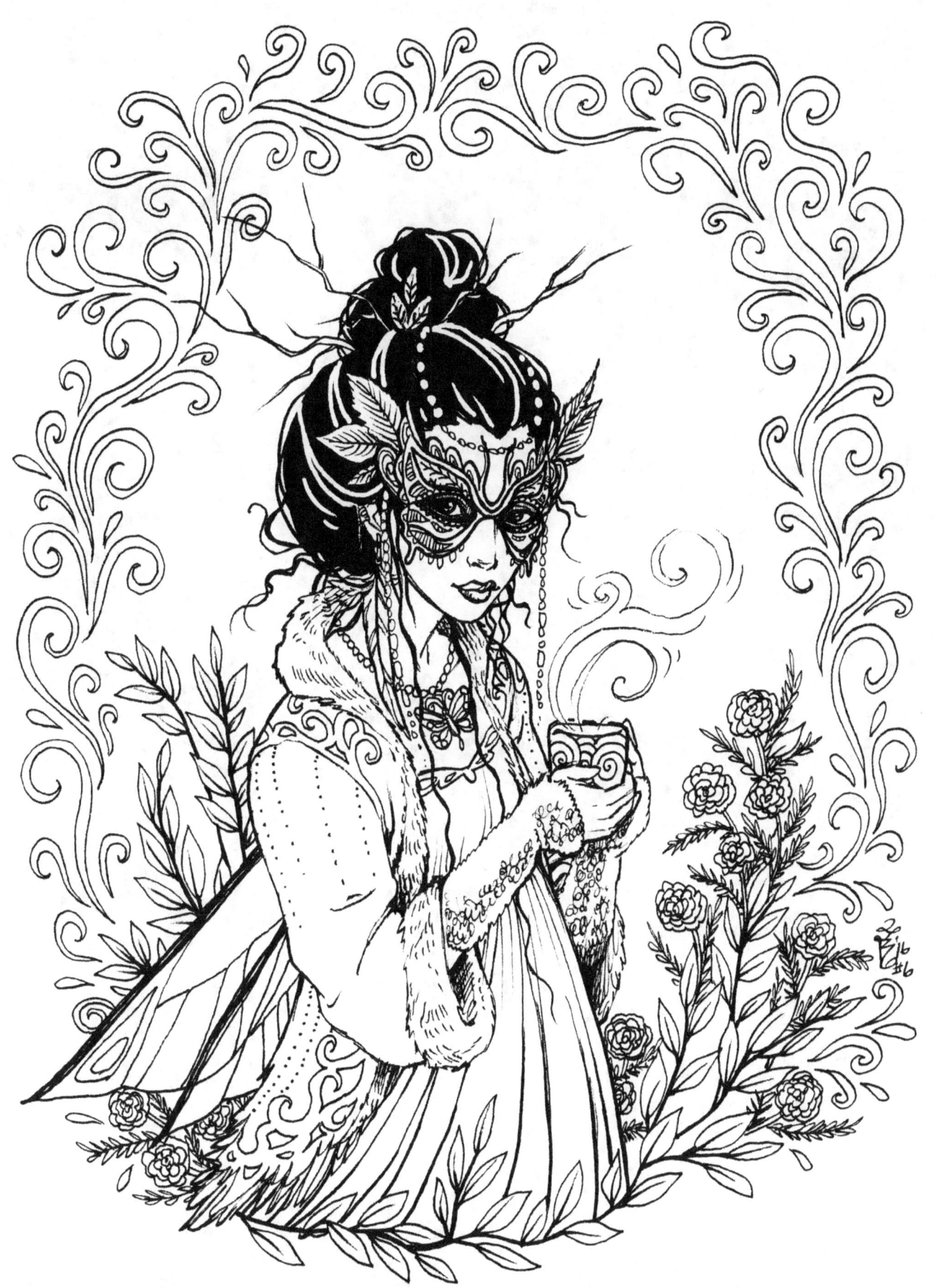

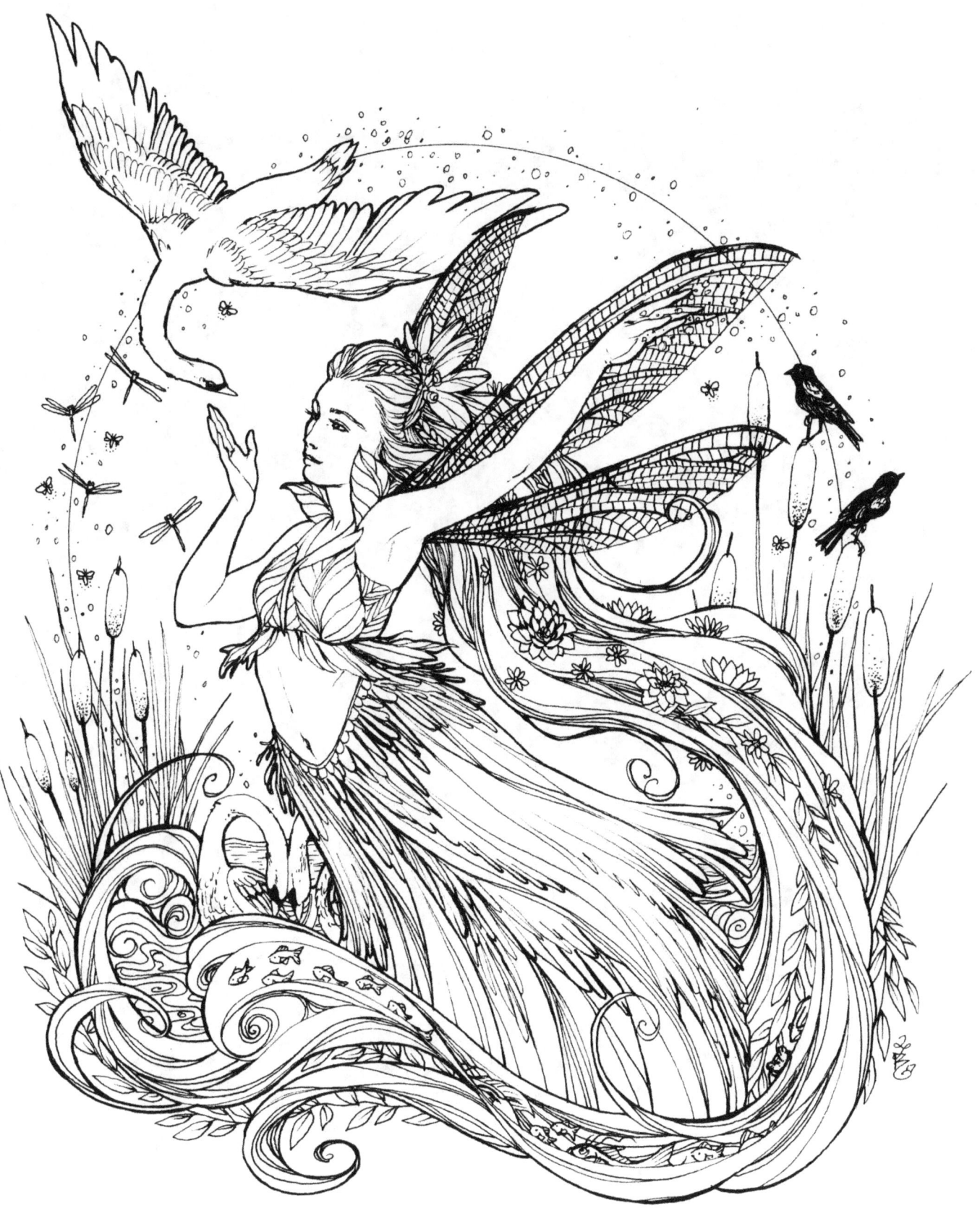

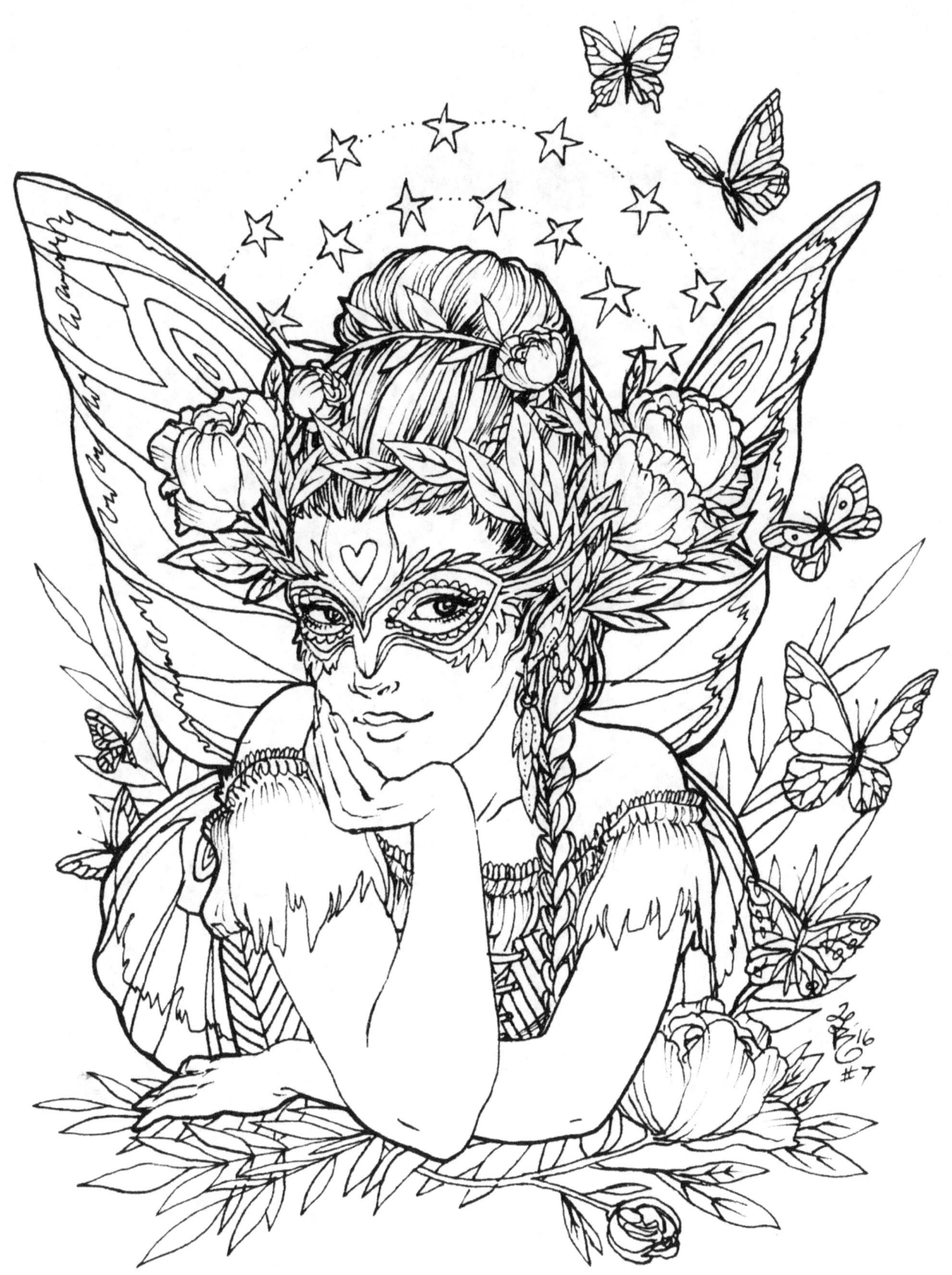

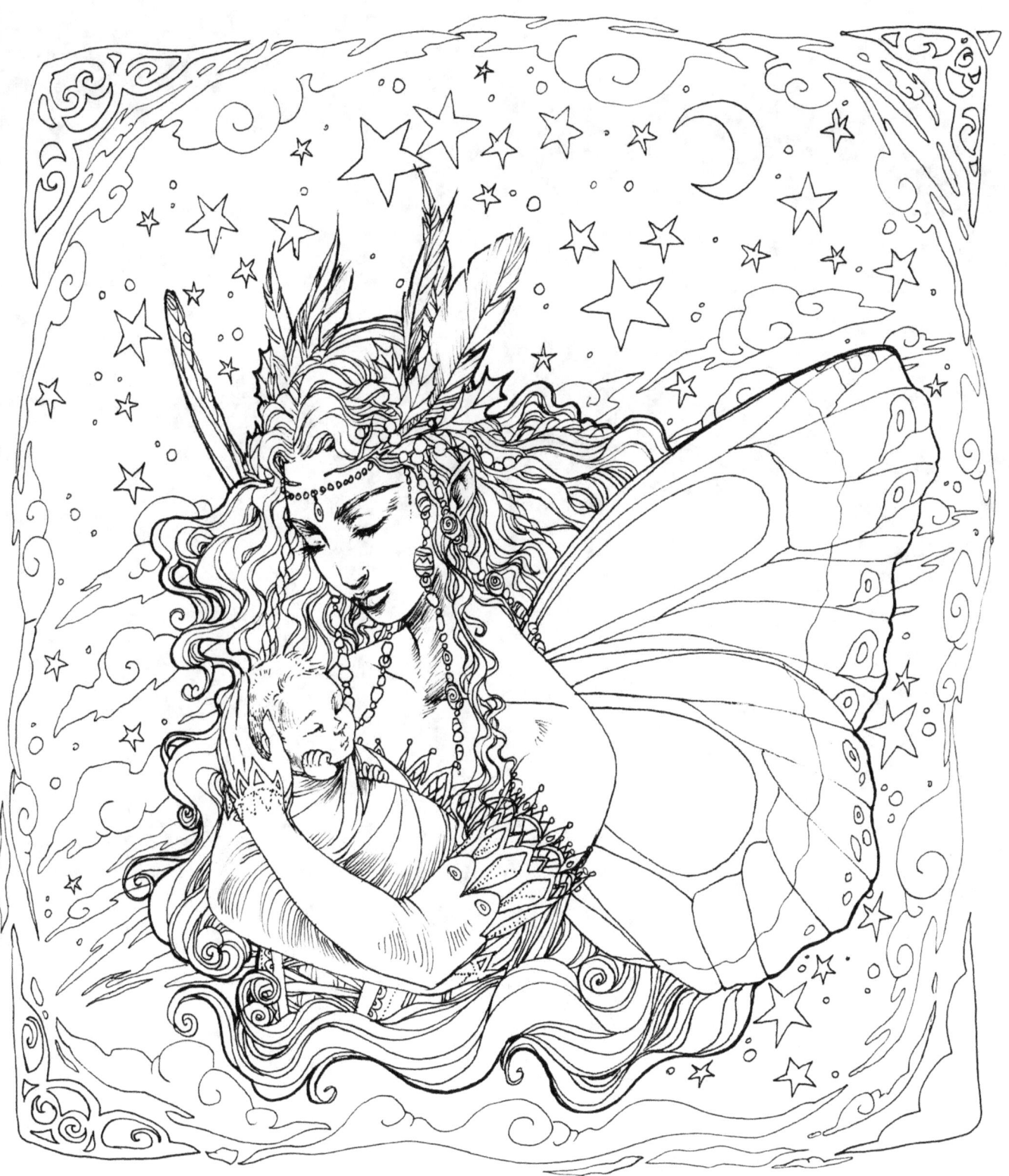

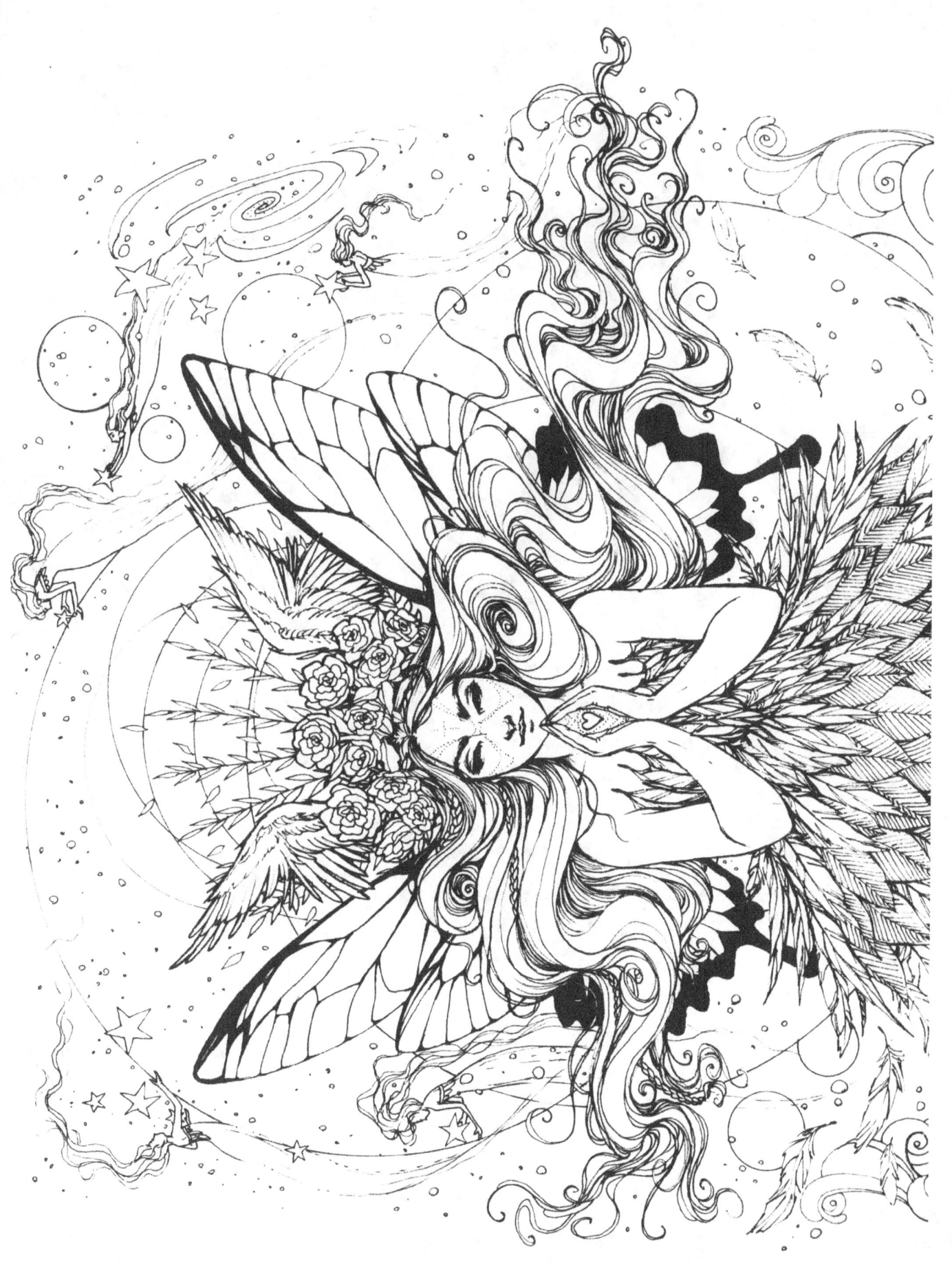

www.ingramcontent.com/pod-product-compliance
Lightning Source LLC
Chambersburg PA
CBHW081622220526
45468CB00010B/2988